It Does Not

Julia Suarez

It Does Not

Poems

Julia Suarez

Bright Hill Press

2006
Treadwell, New York

It Does Not

Poems by Julia Suarez

Selected by Bright Hill Press
Bright Hill Press
At Hand Poetry Chapbook Series, No. 19

Cover Photograph & Book Design: Bertha Rogers
Author Photograph: Ira Soller
Editor in Chief: Bertha Rogers
Editorial Assistant: Lawrence E. Shaw
Copyright © 2006 by Julia Suarez — First Edition

Library of Congress Cataloging-in-Publication Data

Suarez, Julia.
   It does not : poems / Julia Suarez.
      p. cm. -- (At hand poetry chapbook series ; no. 19)
   ISBN 1-892471-39-6 (alk. paper)
   I. Title.
 PS3619.U33I83 2006
 811'.6--dc22

                         2006032943
It Does Not is published by Bright Hill Press, Inc., a not-for-
profit, 501 (c) (3) literary and educational organization founded
in 1992. The organization is registered with the New York
State Department of State, Office of Charities Registration.
Publication of *It Does Not* is made possible, in part, with public
funds from the Literature Program of the New York State
Council on the Arts, a State Agency.
Editorial Address: Bright Hill Press, Inc., 94 Church Street, POB
193, Treadwell, NY 13846-0193. Voice: 607-829-5055; Fax: 607-
829-5054. Web site: brighthillpress.org; E-mail: wordthur@stny.
rr.com.

Aknowledgments

Grateful acknowledgment is made to *Salmagundi*,
where "Small Town" and "Two" were first published.

Julia Suarez

Contents

     Julia Suarez

For my grandmother, Julia Domann Krause,
(1902-1984)

Julia Suarez

It Does Not

move like water. It scours,
obliterating the edges, clean

lines of bodies and faces, angles
of stone bridges, corners

of book covers, blunting teeth and taste.
It makes the heart ache as if it pumped

blood mixed with sand and each
loss etched deeper. It does not

heal: it irradiates, inviting sticks
and jabs. Everything is fuel.

It has no fullness, except what it takes,
cannot be kept or reclaimed. Having no

allegiance, it runs out, yet won't
be cheated.

Julia Suarez

Fit Subjects For An Elegy

First, The Garden State. The gardens
of The Garden State, the night sky
over those gardens. Stars and the death
of stars we have not yet seen. Then

what cannot be replaced: the cut glass heart
my grandmother gave me that I promised
to cherish, then dropped on the street
when I took it outside to see it
catch the sun. The sun it caught.
Her Victrola records, brittle as slates,
I did not catch when they slipped
through my fingers to the cellar floor.
Caruso and Fanny Brice, shattered.

The roadside dead,
opossums, skunks, raccoons
and squirrels crumpled along the asphalt shoulders
like scraps of velvet. Stiff-legged buoys
of deer·bloating on medians. Woodchucks
overturned in the dust. My murdered student,
strangled, raped, her body
dumped in a quarry off the Interstate thirty years ago.

The last unblighted elm. The only person
who remembers my mother when she was a baby.
Slang from the 1920's. Hats.
My grandfather's fedora, my mother's pillbox.
One stone left upon one stone of the temple.
The names of the dead in your mouth.

Julia Suarez

The Shape That Absence Takes

Little bowl the sparrow's breast
makes in the dust this hot day,
a measure of shadow. Up close, curves
her wings left; somewhere

she waits for twilight. In spring
I could see where the snowbanks lay,
long sleepers, their imprint clear
in the deep grass of slopes until

the first good rains. Now, in the empty
house I touch what you touched,
the brass doorknobs, the kitchen handles,
stand precisely where you made

the bed, or hung the laundry
from the back window.
It is impossible
for two bodies to occupy

the same space, I have been told,
impossible that after twenty years
I should find so much as a hair—yet
my eyes go back and back through

decades of redecoration to the designs
of wallpaper I traced with my fingers
in the early hours when I lay still,
waiting for you to call me

down to breakfast in the yellow
kitchen that is beige now and broken and
looks out on the garden that is not there—
I begin to see the places needlepoints

and photos hung and
in the dining room,
where my picture was,
the nail hole in the plaster.

Julia Suarez

Rubric of
My Grandmother's Garden

Ploughed under, uprooted, cut back,
black beds unmade, reorder the order
scattered and lost. Who unmakes a garden?

Hibiscus, Astilbe, Lupine,
Speedwell, Sweet William, Delphinium.

Yours the first garden, the garden I return to.

Cranesbill and Columbine, Dianthus,
Stonecrop and Harebell, Liatris.

You in your apron and open-toed shoes,
I stood high as your hand while you arced
the hose in twilight, and we watered.

Bee Balm and Bleeding Heart, Lambs Ears,
Four 'o Clocks, Lavender, and Loosestrife.

Easily. So easily.
Everything remembered can be forgotten.

Lily of the Valley, Moon Flower, Anemone,
Tall Bearded Iris and Love-in-a-Mist.

Scent of wet blossoms, drenched leaves,
rising, your presence in familiar rooms.
Cut glass vase for the parlor bouquet.

Day Lily, Morning Glory, Gloriosa Daisy,
Marigold and Mignonette, Sunflower.

My soul said, "Everything forgotten can be called back."

There was a snake, but he was little,
like one of the garters Grandpa
wore to hold up his black socks.

Sweet Pea and Poppy, Primrose and Phlox,
Buttercup, Cosmos, and Aster.

"Does a fox wear Foxgloves?" I asked you.

Cockscomb, Chrysanthemum, O, Sweet
Alyssum and Sweet Pea, Baby's Breath,

Peace Rose, come back. I have made a garden.

My kingdom for your Hollyhocks,
your mounded blue Hydrangea!

Julia Suarez

Making the Bed

So here I am in early June, breaking
sod, tearing clumps out with both hands,
trying to get the silver maples to unclench
the rocks and dirt they've clutched a century
then lugging in more dirt and rotted leaves
and cow manure in 40-pound bags and
splitting shale to build a wall so I can make
the only place the sun hits at all a garden.

And you have gone and died on me, you
who had been through every moment of this
life since I first drew breath —
far away and unbeknownst — when I was
sitting on a stone wall last October eating
a Northern Spy and thinking how you liked
them best for pies and luxuriating in the golden
air, wanting to tell you how clear and fine
the fall days were, knowing you must miss them,
down there in New Jersey where you had your
   garden.

When I was a child I used to stay with you all day
outside while you worked weeding, pinching, tying
back, transplanting in your flower beds. When we
were tired, we swung in the hammock, you singing

to me about the garden, stringing all the old-fashioned
flower names into songs that went on and on, *ageratum,*
bachelor's button, columbine, nasturtium, until
I drifted off, wrapped in the heavy woven hammock
like a chrysalis until suppertime when beads of late
light forced themselves between the fibers and I woke.

After supper when the dishes were washed and put
   away,
we came out in the cool of the day to cut a bouquet and
to water. You stood, arcing the hose, so a fine spray
drifted over all, and the heavy blossoms were not
   broken.
And it made perfect sense to me that God, too, had
   enjoyed
walking in His garden and I used to expect Him, there,
among the tallest flowers, and I was afraid.
But you were not, not of anything that frightened me,
the praying mantes with their spiked feet, the bees, or
   even
the quick snake. Not thunder, or the close dark
that came on high summer nights.
I am making this garden. I'm the one who's planting

and pulling and transplanting now, the one who
   drags out the hose
these hot days and stands silently watching water
weight the blossoms, realizing as twilight comes
that I have spent the entire day in the garden
once again. I need to ask you about the foxgloves.
At night, my arms are tired and my head is heavy
with the names of flowers, *nasturtium, campanula,*
   achillea,
and when I tell them like beads, I know again how it
   was
when the hollyhocks were taller than I, and you
were young, and death was like the praying mantes
I would watch and eventually let walk up and down
   my arm.

Coming Home, September 11, 2001

The trees on the south side of my house
still stand. That afternoon

I sat on the back porch steps
and listened: No planes, few cars.

Only the traffic of birds, the transactions
of leaves. My garden was growing. No early frost

had cut it down this season. The second planting
of yellow beans faced full sun. On the shingles

below the dining room window a praying mantis
with his spiked feet; the first I'd seen

in years. I helped him into the flowerbed, where
he'd find something to eat, I told him, and he'd be

safe. Through the window I could see the old life,
framed. My grandmother's armchair and brass lamp

deep in their usual conversations. I saw us
as we were when I was a child and my grandmother

was my age. We would work all morning among her flowers, tending the beds, then

come in for lunch before the worst of the heat.

First Night
December 24, 1979

How the mind slips down a little
avenue and won't come back: the clock

crawls across the hours, each tick
etching itself along my spine. "I've lost

my husband," my grandmother says,
as if she had wandered, letting go

his hand, and for the first time in sixty years
he isn't there. We persuade her to come home,

giving her my parents' bed that she would share
with me, the visiting unmarried daughter.

I am afraid to touch her, her immense
grief, afraid my touch will

hurt, but she turns to me, opening
against my chest not like a flower,

but a shellfish, held so rigidly, I think
she's wearing her corset, all the stays

and bands, the complicated
lacing—but it is *herself*—I hold her and

Julia Suarez

hold her all night. Hear every
breath. The clock.

At last, the first birds sing.
She sleeps, lets go, her head

so small against my shoulder, so small and
resting.

Documentary

This is Walter Cronkite
*and **You** are there.*

Corregidor. Guam. The Marianas.
Grainy footage of the recent war.

We watch in my grandparents' living room,
my parents, my sisters, and my Uncle John,

who *was*. He never spoke
of his time in the Seabees. We knew

he'd lost most of his little finger
building a bridge. They came under attack,

had to pull back fast, his finger
smashed between two pontoons.

He could make us think he'd just
popped off the missing part,

like we popped pop-beads. Would wiggle
the stump as if it were a sausage or a docked

Julia Suarez

tail (this, with sound effects and faces)
to make us laugh, and we three

little girls, because we liked him, did.
Nearly sixty years until he told us

about the battles, the wounded lying
out all night, calling for someone to come;

bodies of men he knew, face down
for days in green water; burial detail.

He says some days the stench
comes back. He can't eat.

His finger aches.
Especially when he shovels snow.

Down

I told you I never liked escalators;
that I avoid them, and you
laughed. The steep

ones that seem to head straight
into the earth—in New York's Port Authority,
or the London Underground. Their

chug, their irreversible
downwardness, constant
stepping. You can't

get off. It began when I was a child:
My grandmother took me to a department store
whose wooden escalator moving its slotted steps

was so like the skeleton
neck of the brontosaurus we'd seen at the Museum
the day before, it was as if the creature were

swallowing. I froze—sure my foot
would slide between those vertebrae and I would be
churned away from her

forever. In the press of shoppers, she
stepped on, turning to take my hand—but some
body came between, and she

Julia Suarez

was gone, passing over the crest of the wooden
   treads as if
taken by a waterfall. I called to her, but she
couldn't come back. Her face grew smaller

as the steps moved her along until she passed
beneath the neon display of a gigantic
coffee pot pouring itself steaming into a lit-up cup

that never filled. She disappeared. I have watched her
vanish night after night
just before I pass into sleep. Her face grows smaller

and smaller, like a child's—and your face is with
hers, small now, too. I watch until I can't make out
your features anymore, only the empty treads
   stepping down.

How Like A Sleeper

How like a sleeper the doe lay
dead along the interstate in the heat,

very golden in the full light
and beginning to bloat, her chin

on the concrete, her belly white, her injuries
concealed from me as I drove

past her, wondering at her beauty and her
unaccustomed stillness. She would

never hold this way in life, would never
think to rest her chin on concrete or let

the day play over her, as if she were safe
and there were no such thing as speeding

heedless cars. If I too, had not been
speeding, intent on my way, I would

have stopped, wanting to stroke her, finally having
my chance to look into a deer's eye,

and touch her lashes, study her face, her muzzle
and fine ears. They say those hooves slash

Julia Suarez

sharp as razors, when she strikes out in fear
for her life, for her young—cloven feet—

the marks they leave in snow and soft earth
deep, and deepening as they age, eye holes

black into another world. Yes, I would stop
and touch her, if I could. But in life, nothing

holds still. The balky child who will not let
you hold her, in sleep, when she does not know

you hover, allows your touch, your eyes
upon her; you can watch until she wakes.

Still Life

Holding the tip of my dog's tail to guide me
in the semi-dark, I follow him

down the stairs and out into the yard. Crushed
paths show me where the deer come down,

does and fawns, cresting the chest-high green.
In swirls they force tall grass aside,

leaving their own crop circles.
Here, one startles, veers and fords the hillside

in another place. Here, the young rest on folded knees
while the doe, knowing motionlessness and
    invisibility

are akin, stands.
And I hold still, remembering the roil of water

around my ankles and what it is to go
so softly the good neighbors, even the birds,

don't know we're here.

Julia Suarez

Saturday Mornings

Into the gully between the backs of Mama and Papa,
on Saturday mornings we would climb and lie

in that place that was like the line along the shore
where the waves break. Papa, a wave turned over,

broad shoulders wrapped in white sheet surf, Mama's
  hair
tangled on a pillow of foam, their rising falling
  breaths—

a rhythm of *not yet*   *let us sleep*   *a little longer*, and we
drawn back into a school-less drowse, this, the only
  morning stretched

out for miles: no work, no bells, no forgotten lunches,
  no world
for a few moments longer but this, each of us in our
  separate

sleeping, a pod of seals, a floating constellation.

Repair

for Jim Couden

Three times, now, the ants have built back
their little Vesuvius I washed out

with boiling water. The hornet,
I see, persists beneath my window:

paper cells grow in clusters
daily like grey roses.

Over the withered stalks of tulips
and hyacinths, perennials flare.

Now, in late June, the garden has
no barren place. Suddenly

the hillsides are fully
green, every tree in leaf.

I didn't think a season of such
fullness could come again;

that it was possible to repair
the world; but you, I suppose,

Julia Suarez

knew better. You would work
in winter on that wooden boat,

the one you were always readying
for summer—we'll scatter

your ashes out beyond the point.
Now, we listen to some jazz

you liked, *"Is That All
There Is?"* We tell each other

"Jim would like that."

On What Would Have Been
Herman Melville's 183rd Birthday

Cape Codders try to rescue pilot whales
who've beached themselves in tourist waters, led
  astray

by their own pilot. In the shallows
they will die unless the locals, linked

in bucket brigade, can keep their fragile
skins wet until the tide comes in.

Their bodies cannot sustain their own
weight without the grace of water—

must float lest they crush their own
organs as they lie suffocating

in the heat. Even with the willing hands
to help them into deep water, many

will die and more, once freed,
will misguide themselves again

on to another bar of sand, where most
will be euthanized by the good people

     Julia Suarez

who say they could not stand by
and watch other "sentient beings"

suffer. Old Whaler, how many
of our own we've watched, this way, wavering,

unable—or unwilling—to help
back into life or over into the other.

Small Town

A man mildly interested in the woman
whose path he crosses for twenty years

asks her to have coffee. She, bone tired
of the nights, capitulates. They are not

jolted from their orbits by desire, but
here there is no other and she marries

the habit of him rather than continue
as she is. She says they make

a comfortable life. The same,
the daily presentation of the same,

the compass of the possible—my neighbor's
bald head at the breakfast table, the sheen

of it, bent to his coffee, rises out the window
like my morning star. Sometimes I pray

for a major disturbance in my heavens—he is
always there, both of us

in our places. All those deep
mid-winter mornings before dawn,

Julia Suarez

both of us shoveling our way out,
down in our trenches, hefting the latest

accumulation where we hailed
each other in the spring, mowing

grass—always he clears in the same
pattern, first the porch steps, then

a path to the drive: I will remember these
particulars when larger things have worn away,

when I lose the threads of important
conversations. I will remember

how his wife always asks about the flowers
that open late afternoons and drift

their scent through her kitchen—asks me
every summer when they bloom, what

they are, and forgets and asks and forgets
again and remarks how sweet they smell.

Four O'Clocks, I say.

Remembered Horses

Walking, they come to me down
a lane thirty years long: Jaguar,
The Chestnut, sixteen hands; Roxanne
of the four spike eyelashes, slow
to anger, slower to respond, bay;
Quizas, slighter, tentative, and lithe,
perhaps today he would do my bidding,
and La Contessa, midnight silk, star
dapple forehead, light foot, trembling
beneath my uneasy touch. Once
she ran with me and would not stop
until I made her circle, smaller, smaller
and she stood one heartbeat in the center
of the field, a black dart struck
to the bulls eye, then took off
flashing for she-knew-where—

I clenched her long mane
hung on until my fingers
opened and she flung me
into brambles, where I stuck, elbow
through my favorite shirt, face
bleeding. She gleamed at me,
lowered her head to me. Let
me on. I dream of her, her brilliant
skin, her velvet gait. So long ago,

Julia Suarez

she is dust. She is speed, my
sixteenth summer, sweet nightmare.

Two

Body finds Spirit not open to negotiations, not
willing to dicker, deal, come to consensus:

they cannot eat at the same restaurant—no
choosing one from column A, one from B;

can't even agree on a table. At best, an uneasy
alliance, unlikely bedfellows doing a Tarantella

on the head of a pin—that's about all the common
ground they share: for Spirit, The *Ten*

Commandments are a package deal, all Ten
or none. Belief is no smorgasbord. Body

wants an easement now and then, a forgiving
barrier around The Garden of Earthly Delights,

a not-too-careful headcount at the end of the day.
Spirit is stringent, Body (forever fooled by its

insubstantial appearance) mistakes it for mere
breath. And Spirit errs when it forgets

the tenacity of blood and bone, how insistent
the grip of the tight-fisted heart; that Body

does not aspire, but survives, and Spirit must
be embodied, however cracked the vessel. Body

gorges, Spirit has a finer palate. Body lusts
and aches and does not understand its urges; Spirit

loves and aches and worships its beloved, laying down
itself, the very jewel Body does not know it wants.

The Angel At The End
from a drawing by George Mesologites

The angel who came for me
had muscular arms—a good wrestler—
capable of rolling pastry dough
thin as Bible pages, or rolling up
her great sleeves to turn
a celestial calf laid wrong
in the birth canal of heaven.
Nothing diaphanous about her; instead,

a kind of quilted overcoat, marvelously
wrought with stitches, some of them
I seem to have taken myself,
depicting scenes from my life—
everything, as if I had been
some Egyptian notable followed by my scribe.
Recent events worked around the border,
near the hem; yesterday trailing
the very bottom, even the words
I planned, my eloquent plea—O
Great One, grant me time! Some
curlicues about potential, misspent youth.
I could see the corner where the stitching
stopped—I asked her if she'd cut the thread.
She put her head beside my head and drew
one gigantic wing around my shoulder.

Julia Suarez

Around A Small Lake In April

Dissolved back into this day, day I remember,
day I have lived over and over, always an April day
like this, by bright water, full sun.

Beneath the surface the blue steel edge,
and in the shadows, cold stones. Cold to come,
and the plunge to darkness, even after this light.

I listen.

Now my ears are full of light, cups of sun.

Now birdsong.

The same bird
has been singing to me all these years.

He is the teacher, solicitous and wise.
He sings *Take these notes   now*
*again. You   are   not   **listening***—I have never seen him

but I know the shape of his sleek head as he nods,
bright-eyed, bending to see if I have heard. I am so
   slow.
Maybe this time, maybe this season—*try   again:*
You   will   understand.

My hair, blowing across my face
shines as sunlight moves up and down each shaft like
   water.

When this newness (this old newness) does not make
   me new again,
where will I go?

About the Author

Julia (Julie) Suarez is an Assistant Professor of English and Writing Center Coordinator at Hartwick College, her alma mater, in Oneonta, New York. Raised in the Garden State, she finds her own garden an endless source of inspiration and a constant link to family and childhood. Her first chapbook, *The Lesser Light,* was published by Swamp Press in 1981. Poems have most recently appeared in *Salmagundi, Phoebe, Big City Lit,* and *BLINK.* She has studied at the New York State Summer Writers Institute for many years. In 1992 she won the Upper Catskill Community Council of the Arts Regional Writing Competition in poetry and has received several grants to research and transcribe historic journals.

About the Book

The type and layout for *It Does Not* were designed by Bertha Rogers, as was the cover. The typefaces for the text are Adobe InDesign Palatino Linotype Book Type. The typeface for the cover is Adobe InDesign Bell Book Type. The book was printed on 60-lb. offset, acid-free, recycled paper in the United States of America. This first edition is limited to copies in paper wrappers.

About Bright Hill Press

OUR MISSION: To seek out, study, and collect the work of early and contemporary writers, storytellers, and artists, and to publish, disseminate, and present that work through publications and educational and public programs for the larger community.

OUR HISTORY: Bright Hill Press/Word Thursdays was founded in 1992 by Bertha Rogers, with the assistance of Ernest M. Fishman. A writer, teacher, and visual artist, Ms. Rogers serves as the organization's executive director and editor in chief. Mr. Fishman has served BHP as president and/or chief financial officer since its beginnings. Bright Hill Press is located at Bright Hill Center, 94 Church Street, in the hamlet of Treadwell, in New York's Catskill Mountain Region; program participants are from Delaware, Otsego, Sullivan, Schoharie, Broome, and Chenango counties as well. Programs and services have grown to meet the stated and implied needs of both youth and adult populations in those counties, as well as the needs of the literary community in New York State and beyond. BHP's current administrative focus is on long-range planning, in order to better fulfill its mission and expand its programs.

OUR ARTISTIC PHILOSOPHY: Bright Hill Press is dedicated to increasing audiences' appreciation of the writing arts and oral traditions that comprise American literature, and to encouraging and furthering the tradition of oral poetry and writing in the Catskills. Writers and artists who participate in BHP's programs are selected for their artistic excellence, their ability and willingness to work within a community setting, and the diversity of their backgrounds, genres, and styles. BHP understands that recognition of the need for a literary community and a commitment to lifelong learning are critical aspects of audience development; the organization's programs for children and adults engender the spirit, craft, and imagination that make this possible.

OUR PROGRAMS are offered to people of all ages. Current program offerings include:

WORD THURSDAYS, a reading series begun in 1992 and presenting open readings followed by readings and discussion by featured authors;

BRIGHT HILL BOOKS, publishing anthologies as well as chapbooks and poetry collections by individual authors since 1994;

BRIGHT HILL LIBRARY & INTERNET WING, since 2004, a facility with more than 6,000 titles of prose and poetry, art, reference, nature, and children's books for the immediate and larger community;

NEW YORK STATE'S LITERARY WEB SITE, nyslittree.org (since 1999), and the New York State Literary Map (in print and online), developed and administered by BHP, in partnership with the New York State Council on the Arts;

WORD THURSDAYS SHARE THE WORDS HS Poetry Mentoring Program and Competition, affording young poets a chance to write and present their own poetry in a public competition since 1996;

WORD THURSDAYS LITERARY WORKSHOPS FOR KIDS & ADULTS, offering, since 1994, innovative programs that celebrate and incorporate the elegant use of words with other disciplines;

WORD & IMAGE GALLERY, dedicated, since 2002, to presenting works by regional and national artists that integrate words and images;

PATTERNS, BHC's New Literary Garden/Park for the whole community, landscaped and created by Catskill Outdoor Educational Corps, a program of Americorps at SUNY Delhi;

BHC INTERNSHIP PROGRAM for College and HS Students, offering, since 1994, students an opportunity to learn the business of literature;

GOVERNANCE: Bright Hill Press/Word Thursdays is an independent 501 (c) (3), not-for-profit corporation governed by a board of directors representing the community the organization series, and an advisory board from the larger community.

Bright Hill Press At Hand
Poetry Chapbook Series

Bright Hill Press At Hand
Poetry Chapbook Series *(forthcoming titles)*

A Sense of Place, Bhikshuni Weisbrot, 2007
(2005 Poetry Chapbook Award)
hairpin loop, Anne Blonstein, 2007
The Coriolis Effect, Michael Dowdy, 2007
The Courtship & Other Tales, Kathryn Ugoretz, 2007

Bright Hill Press
Poetry Book Award Series

The Artist As Alice: From A Photographer's Life
Darcy Cummings, 2006, $14
2004 Poetry Book Award
Chosen by Carolyne Wright

The Aerialist
Victoria Hallerman, 2005, $12
2003 Poetry Book Award
Chosen by Martin Mitchell

Strange Gravity
Lisa Rhoades, 2004, $12
2002 Poetry Book Award
Chosen by Elaine Terranova

The Singer's Temple
Barbara Hurd, 2003, $12
2001 Poetry Book Award
Chosen by Richard Frost

Julia Suarez

Bright Hill Press
Poetry Book Award Series (cont.)

Heart, with Piano Wire
Richard Deutch, 2002, $12
2000 Poetry Book Award
Chosen by Maurice Kenny

My Father & Miro & Other Poems
Claudia M. Reder, 2001, $12
1999 Poetry Book Award
Chosen by Colette Inez

Traveling Through Glass
Beth Copeland Vargo, 2000, $12
1998 Poetry Book Award
Chosen by Karen Swenson

To Fit Your Heart into the Body
Judith Neeld, 1999, $12
1997 Poetry Book Award
Chosen by Richard Foerster

Blue Wolves
Regina O'Melveny, 1997, $12
1996 Poetry Book Award
Chosen by Michael Waters

My Own Hundred Doors
Pam Bernard, 1996, $10
1996 Poetry Book Award
Chosen by Carol Frost

Bright Hill Press Anthologies

Speaking the Words Anthology, 1994

The Word Thursdays Anthology of Poetry & Fiction, 1995

The Second Word Thursdays Anthology:
Poetry & Prose by Bright Hill Press Writers, 1999

On the Watershed: The Natural World
of New York's Catskill Mountain Region/
Poetry & Prose by Catskill Student Writers, 2001

Bright Hill Press Word & Image Series

Breathing the Monster Alive, Eric Gansworth 2006

Emmet Till & Other Stories, Per Frykdahl
(forthcoming, 2007)

Out of the Catskills & Just Beyond
Literary & Visual Works by Catskill Writers & Artists, 1997

Iroquois Voices, Iroquois Visions
A Celebration of Contemporary Six Nations Arts, 1996

Julia Suarez

Bright Hill Press Exhibition Series

Bright Hill Book Arts 2006 $16
Edited by Bertha Rogers

Bright Hill Book Arts 2005 $16
Edited by Bertha Rogers with Edward Hutchins

Bright Hill Book Arts 2004 $12
Edited by Bertha Rogers

Bright Hill Book Arts 2003 $10
Edited by Bertha Rogers

Bright Hill Book Arts 2002 $10
Edited by Bertha Rogers